This book club journal belongs to:

_____

Book Club Calendar

Month: _____

BOOK:

DATE:

LOCATION:

HOST:

Month: _____

BOOK:

DATE:

LOCATION:

HOST:

Month: _____

BOOK:

DATE:

LOCATION:

HOST:

Book Club Calendar

Month: _____

BOOK:

DATE:

LOCATION:

HOST:

Month: _____

BOOK:

DATE:

LOCATION:

HOST:

Month: _____

BOOK:

DATE:

LOCATION:

HOST:

Book Club Calendar

Month: _____

BOOK:

DATE:

LOCATION:

HOST:

Month: _____

BOOK:

DATE:

LOCATION:

HOST:

Month: _____

BOOK:

DATE:

LOCATION:

HOST:

Book Club Calendar

Month: _____

BOOK:

DATE:

LOCATION:

HOST:

Month: _____

BOOK:

DATE:

LOCATION:

HOST:

Month: _____

BOOK:

DATE:

LOCATION:

HOST:

Month

_____

MY BOOK CLUB
Reading Journal

TITLE:

AUTHOR:

GENRE:

BOOK CLUB DATE:

STARTED: FINISHED:

RATING: ☆ ☆ ☆ ☆ ☆

RECOMMENDED BY:

OTHER BOOKS BY AUTHOR:

QUOTES AND NOTES

PG: /

PG: /

PG: /

PG: /

PG: /

PG: /

PG: /

PG: /

PG: /

PG: /

PG: /

PG: /

PG: /

PG: /

PG: /

PG: /

Let' s talk about it

Let's talk about it

Month

MY BOOK CLUB
Reading Journal

TITLE:

AUTHOR:

GENRE:

BOOK CLUB DATE:

STARTED:

FINISHED:

RATING: ☆ ☆ ☆ ☆ ☆

RECOMMENDED BY:

OTHER BOOKS BY AUTHOR:

QUOTES AND NOTES

PG: /

PG: /

PG: /

PG: /

PG: /

PG: /

PG: /

PG: /

PG: /

PG: /

PG: /

PG: /

PG: /

PG: /

PG: /

PG: /

Let's talk about it

Let's talk about it

Month

MY BOOK CLUB

Reading Journal

TITLE:

AUTHOR:

GENRE:

BOOK CLUB DATE:

STARTED:

FINISHED:

RATING: ☆ ☆ ☆ ☆ ☆

RECOMMENDED BY:

OTHER BOOKS BY AUTHOR:

QUOTES AND NOTES

PG: /

PG: /

PG: /

PG: /

PG: /

PG: /

PG: /

PG: /

PG: _____ / _____

PG: _____ / _____

PG: _____ / _____

PG: _____ / _____

PG: _____ / _____

PG: _____ / _____

PG: _____ / _____

PG: _____ / _____

Let's talk about it

Let's talk about it

Month

_____

MY BOOK CLUB
Reading Journal

TITLE:

AUTHOR:

GENRE:

BOOK CLUB DATE:

STARTED:

FINISHED:

RATING: ☆ ☆ ☆ ☆ ☆

RECOMMENDED BY:

OTHER BOOKS BY AUTHOR:

QUOTES AND NOTES

PG: /

PG: /

PG: /

PG: /

PG: /

PG: /

PG: /

PG: /

PG: /

PG: /

PG: /

PG: /

PG: /

PG: /

PG: /

PG: /

Let's talk about it

Let's talk about it

Month

_____

MY BOOK CLUB
Reading Journal

TITLE:

AUTHOR:

GENRE:

BOOK CLUB DATE:

STARTED:

FINISHED:

RATING: ☆ ☆ ☆ ☆ ☆

RECOMMENDED BY:

OTHER BOOKS BY AUTHOR:

QUOTES AND NOTES

PG: /

PG: /

PG: /

PG: /

PG: /

PG: /

PG: /

PG: /

PG: _____ / _____

PG: _____ / _____

PG: _____ / _____

PG: _____ / _____

PG: _____ / _____

PG: _____ / _____

PG: _____ / _____

PG: _____ / _____

Let's talk about it

Let's talk about it

Month

_____

MY BOOK CLUB
Reading Journal

TITLE:

AUTHOR:

GENRE:

BOOK CLUB DATE:

STARTED:

FINISHED:

RATING: ☆ ☆ ☆ ☆ ☆

RECOMMENDED BY:

OTHER BOOKS BY AUTHOR:

QUOTES AND NOTES

PG: /

PG: /

PG: /

PG: /

PG: /

PG: /

PG: /

PG: /

PG: _____ / _____

PG: _____ / _____

PG: _____ / _____

PG: _____ / _____

PG: _____ / _____

PG: _____ / _____

PG: _____ / _____

PG: _____ / _____

Let's talk about it

Let's talk about it

Month

_____

MY BOOK CLUB
Reading Journal

TITLE:

AUTHOR:

GENRE:

BOOK CLUB DATE:

STARTED:

FINISHED:

RATING: ☆ ☆ ☆ ☆ ☆

RECOMMENDED BY:

OTHER BOOKS BY AUTHOR:

QUOTES AND NOTES

PG: /

PG: /

PG: /

PG: /

PG: /

PG: /

PG: /

PG: /

MORE QUOTES AND NOTES

PG: _____ / _____

PG: _____ / _____

PG: _____ / _____

PG: _____ / _____

PG: _____ / _____

PG: _____ / _____

PG: _____ / _____

PG: _____ / _____

Let's talk about it

Let's talk about it

Mouth

_____

MY BOOK CLUB
Reading Journal

TITLE:

AUTHOR:

GENRE:

BOOK CLUB DATE:

STARTED:

FINISHED:

RATING: ☆ ☆ ☆ ☆ ☆

RECOMMENDED BY:

OTHER BOOKS BY AUTHOR:

QUOTES AND NOTES

PG: /

PG: /

PG: /

PG: /

PG: /

PG: /

PG: /

PG: /

MORE QUOTES AND NOTES

PG: /

PG: /

PG: /

PG: /

PG: /

PG: /

PG: /

PG: /

Let' s talk about it

Let's talk about it

Mouth

MY BOOK CLUB
Reading Journal

TITLE:

AUTHOR:

GENRE:

BOOK CLUB DATE:

STARTED:

FINISHED:

RATING: ☆ ☆ ☆ ☆ ☆

RECOMMENDED BY:

OTHER BOOKS BY AUTHOR:

QUOTES AND NOTES

PG: /

PG: /

PG: /

PG: /

PG: /

PG: /

PG: /

PG: /

MORE QUOTES AND NOTES

PG: _____ / _____

PG: _____ / _____

PG: _____ / _____

PG: _____ / _____

PG: _____ / _____

PG: _____ / _____

PG: _____ / _____

PG: _____ / _____

Let's talk about it

Let's talk about it

Month

_____

MY BOOK CLUB
Reading Journal

TITLE:

AUTHOR:

GENRE:

BOOK CLUB DATE:

STARTED: FINISHED:

RATING: ☆ ☆ ☆ ☆ ☆

RECOMMENDED BY:

OTHER BOOKS BY AUTHOR:

QUOTES AND NOTES

PG: /

PG: /

PG: /

PG: /

PG: /

PG: /

PG: /

PG: /

PG: _____ / _____

PG: _____ / _____

PG: _____ / _____

PG: _____ / _____

PG: _____ / _____

PG: _____ / _____

PG: _____ / _____

PG: _____ / _____

Let's talk about it

Let' s talk about it

Mouth

_____

MY BOOK CLUB
Reading Journal

TITLE:

AUTHOR:

GENRE:

BOOK CLUB DATE:

STARTED:

FINISHED:

RATING: ☆ ☆ ☆ ☆ ☆

RECOMMENDED BY:

OTHER BOOKS BY AUTHOR:

QUOTES AND NOTES

PG: /

PG: /

PG: /

PG: /

PG: /

PG: /

PG: /

PG: /

PG: /

PG: /

PG: /

PG: /

PG: /

PG: /

PG: /

PG: /

Let's talk about it

Let's talk about it

Month

_____

MY BOOK CLUB
Reading Journal

TITLE:

AUTHOR:

GENRE:

BOOK CLUB DATE:

STARTED: FINISHED:

RATING: ☆ ☆ ☆ ☆ ☆

RECOMMENDED BY:

OTHER BOOKS BY AUTHOR:

QUOTES AND NOTES

PG: /

PG: /

PG: /

PG: /

PG: /

PG: /

PG: /

PG: /

PG: _____ / _____

PG: _____ / _____

PG: _____ / _____

PG: _____ / _____

PG: _____ / _____

PG: _____ / _____

PG: _____ / _____

PG: _____ / _____

Let's talk about it

Let's talk about it

Books to Read Next

Have you read?

BOOKS TO RECOMMEND	AUTHOR

Have you read?

BOOKS TO RECOMMEND	AUTHOR

Have you read?

BOOKS TO RECOMMEND	AUTHOR

Have you read?

BOOKS TO RECOMMEND	AUTHOR

Manufactured by Amazon.ca
Acheson, AB